WORKING TOWARDS
EQUALITY

# What Is
# ANTISEMITISM?

**Monique Polak**

*e* Explore other books at:
WWW.ENGAGEBOOKS.COM

VANCOUVER, B.C.

e → WWW.ENGAGEBOOKS.COM

*What Is Antisemitism? - Working Towards Equality*: Level 3
Polak, Monique 1960 –
Text © 2023 Engage Books
Design © 2023 Engage Books

Edited by: A.R. Roumanis, Ashley Lee, and Melody Sun
Design by: Mandy Christiansen

Text set in Montserrat Regular.
Chapter headings set in Merlo Neue.

FIRST EDITION / FIRST PRINTING

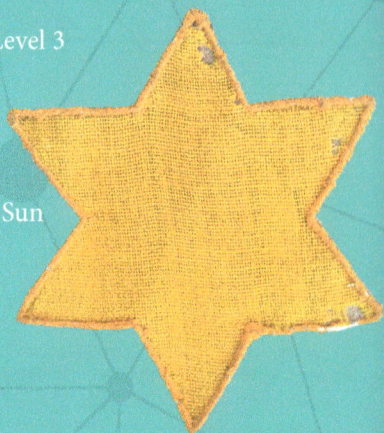

LIBRARY AND ARCHIVES CANADA CATALOGUING IN PUBLICATION

Title: What Is Antisemitism? / Monique Polak.
Names: Polak, Monique, author.
Description: Series statement: Working towards equality

Identifiers: Canadiana (print) 20230447589 | Canadiana (ebook) 20230447597
ISBN 978-1-77476-863-1 (hardcover)
ISBN 978-1-77476-864-8 (softcover)
ISBN 978-1-77476-865-5 (epub)
ISBN 978-1-77476-866-2 (pdf)
ISBN 978-1-77878-129-2 (audio)

Subjects: LCSH: Antisemitism—Juvenile literature.
Classification: LCC DS145 .P435 2023 | DDC J305.892/4—DC23

This project has been made possible in part by the Government of Canada.

Canada

# Contents

# What Is Antisemitism?

Jews believe in one god who gave them the **Torah**. Their religion is called Judaism. It is one of the world's major religions.

**Torah:** books containing God's teachings and laws.

Judaism started in the Middle East nearly 4,000 years ago.

Antisemitism is the hatred of Jews. "Anti" means to be against. "Semitism" refers to Semites, which includes Jews. Semites are people who spoke or speak a Semitic language.

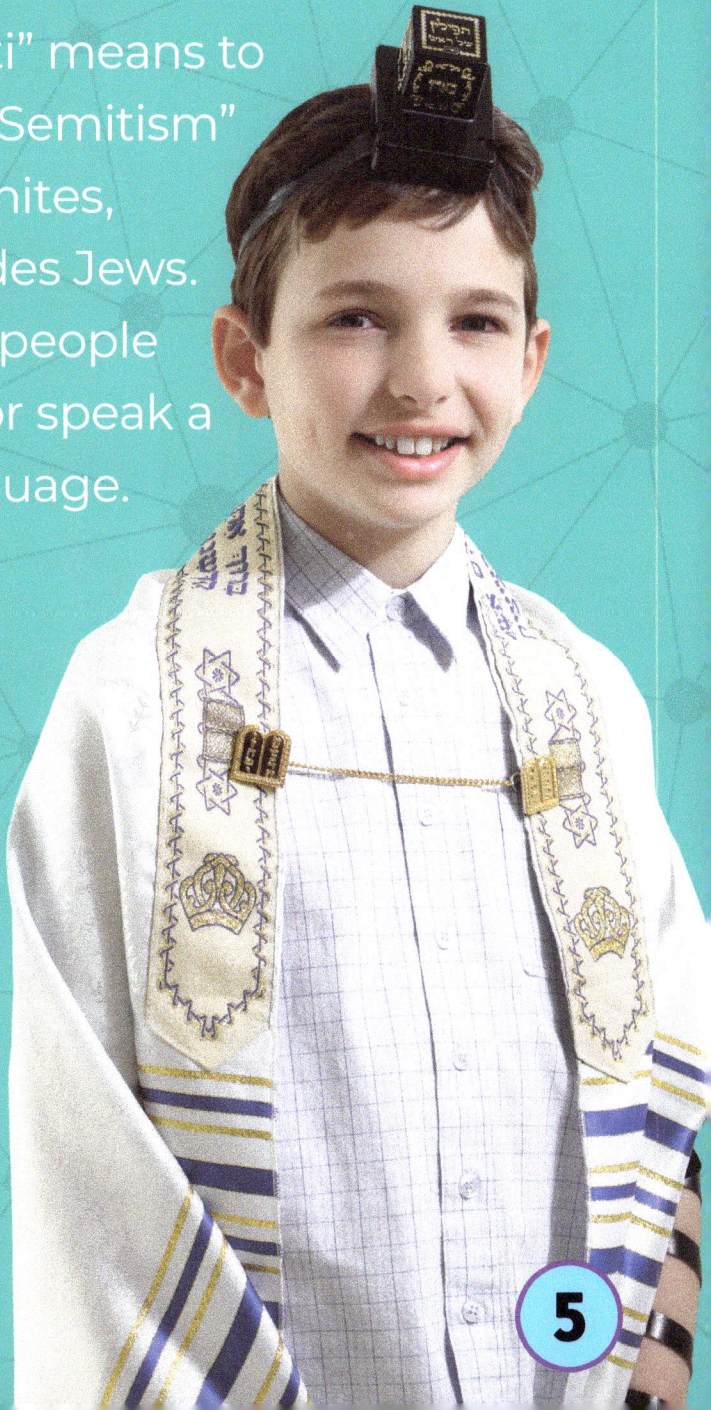

# The History of Antisemitism 1

Antisemitism is thought to be history's oldest hatred. As early as 30 AD, some Christians said that Jews killed Christ. This lie helped antisemitism spread. But Jews have never given up their religion or **customs**.

**Customs:** ways of behaving.

In 1964, Pope Paul VI said Jews did not cause Christ's death. He was the leader of the largest Christian religion.

Many people used to believe that Jews controlled money and banks. During the Middle Ages, Jews in eastern and central Europe were not allowed to own or farm land or join the military. **Lending** money was one of the few jobs they were allowed to do.

**Lending:** giving money to people or businesses that they will pay back later.

As far back as 1824, the word "Jew" was used as an insult to describe someone who likes to hang on to their money.

# The History of Antisemitism 2

Starting in 1516, Jews in European cities were forced to live in poor areas called ghettos. Walls were often built to keep them inside. Ghettos were no longer allowed in the 1800s. They were brought back during World War II.

The term "antisemitism" was first used in the late 1800s by a writer named Wilhelm Marr. Marr wrote about how Jews should not be allowed to be German **citizens**. He believed Jews were planning to take over Germany.

**Citizens:** members of a country.

9

# What Was the Holocaust?

The strongest example of antisemitism is the Holocaust. During World War II, the **Nazis** ruled Germany. Their leader, Adolf Hitler, believed Jews were no better than rats. He wanted to destroy Jews and their customs.

KEYWORD

**Nazis:** members of Hitler's political party.

Many non-Jewish Germans believed Hitler when he called them the master race and said they were better than all other races.

Hitler believed that Jews should be killed. Six million Jews were killed during the Holocaust. Most died in **concentration camps**. Those who lived through the Holocaust are called Holocaust survivors.

**KEY WORD**

**Concentration camps:** places where people were locked up, starved, and forced to live in poor conditions.

11

# Why Are Some People Antisemitic?

No one is born antisemitic. Antisemitic behavior is learned from adults and **peers**. Antisemitism can be spoken, written, or shown through someone's actions.

**KEY WORD**

**Peers:** people in your own age group or social group.

It is easier for people to blame others than to change their own behavior. Jews have been blamed for many things that are not their fault. To put an end to antisemitism, people need to understand how this hatred came to be.

Henry Ford, the American car maker, made many people believe that Jews were the cause of all the world's evils.

# What Does Antisemitism Look Like?

Verbal violence is common. This is when someone uses their words to be mean to others. It often includes yelling. There are even antisemitic **slurs**.

Antisemitic signs, such as "Jews not welcome," are common.

Movies, TV shows, and social media can also be antisemitic. The movie *The Sudden Wealth of the Poor People of Kombach* was made in Germany in 1971. It shows Jews as rich and **devious**.

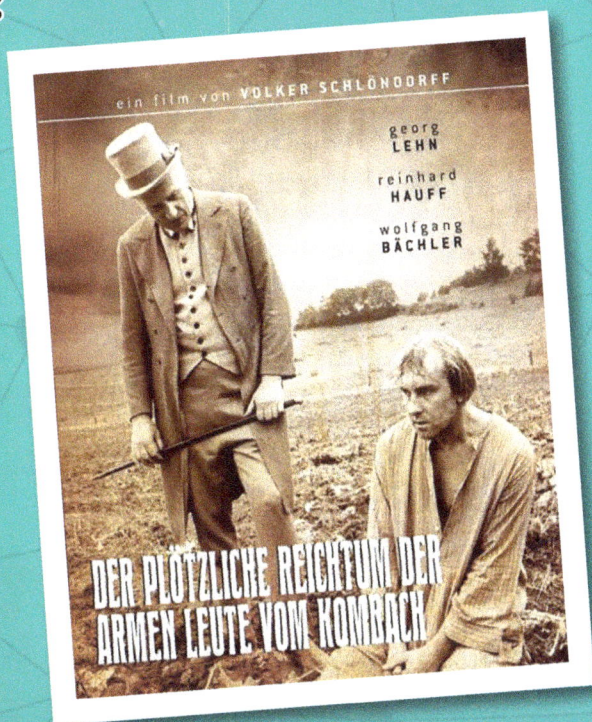

ein film von VOLKER SCHLÖNDORFF

georg LEHN

reinhard HAUFF

wolfgang BÄCHLER

DER PLÖTZLICHE REICHTUM DER ARMEN LEUTE VOM KOMBACH

# Antisemitism Today

The country Israel was created after the Holocaust so Jews could return to their **homeland**. Thousands of Arabs in Palestine were forced to leave their homes that were on that land. To this day, both sides continue to fight.

Many people believe that Israel should not exist.

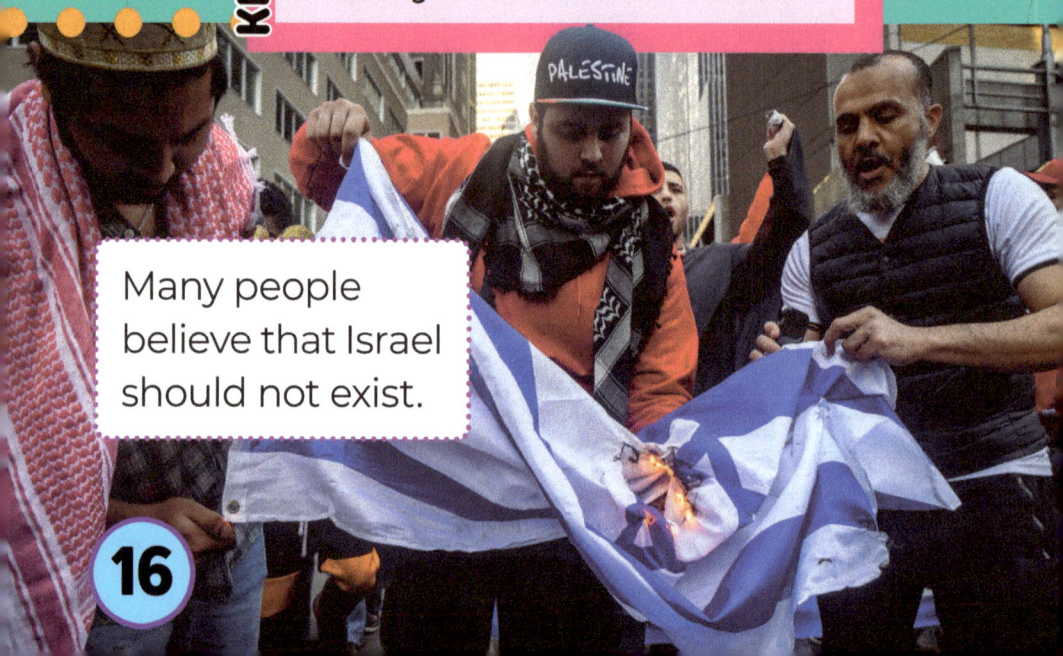

The swastika was a symbol used by the Nazis. It is still found in many places online. Hate groups have decided to use it as their own.

Headstones in Jewish cemeteries are often damaged with drawings of swastikas.

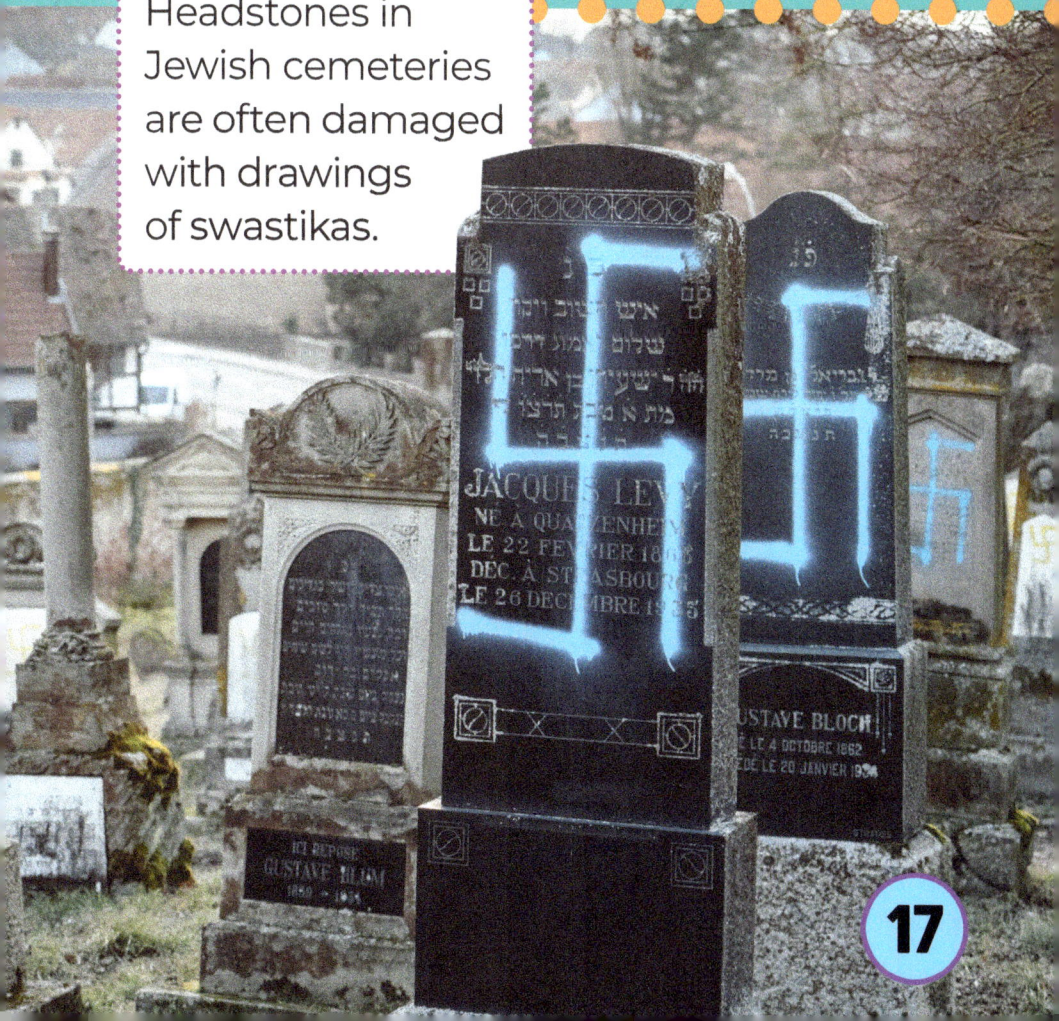

# What to Do if You See or Experience Antisemitism 1

If someone says something antisemitic, you could ask if they know they are being antisemitic. If they say they were joking, tell them that any antisemitic speech is **hate speech**.

KEY WORD

**Hate speech:** public speech that is hateful or encourages violence towards a group of people.

Many countries are putting laws in place to fight online hate speech.

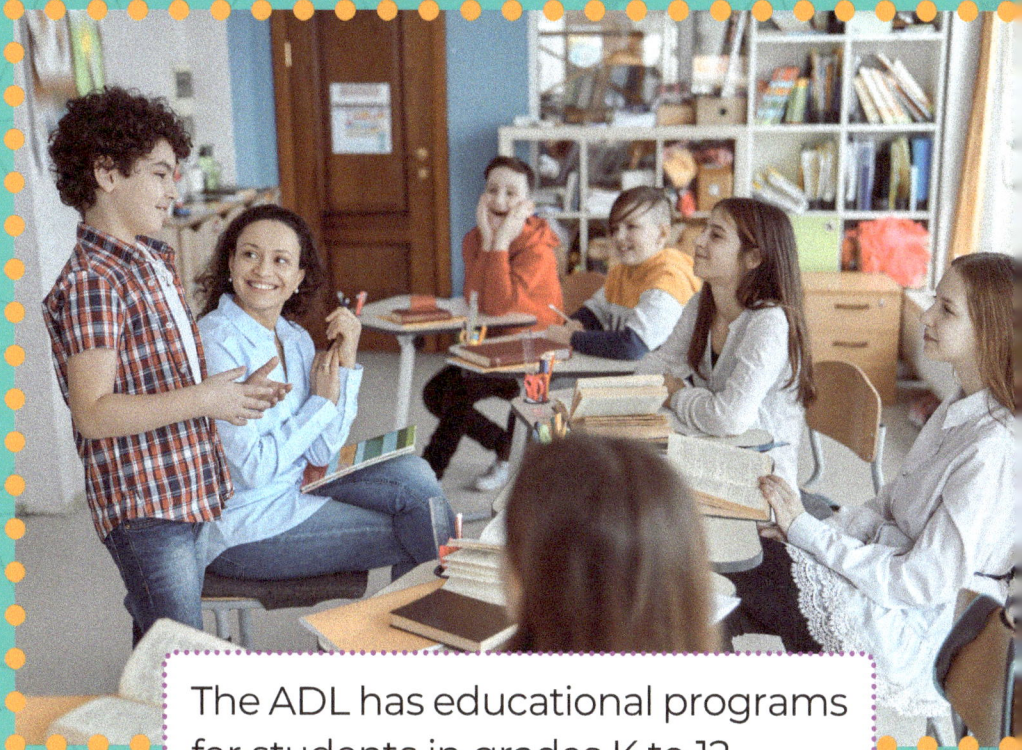

The ADL has educational programs for students in grades K to 12.

Many people do not know about antisemitism. You can help them learn about it. Organizations like the Anti-Defamation League (ADL) and the Jewish Education Project teach people about antisemitism.

# What to Do if You See or Experience Antisemitism 2

If you see antisemitism online, report it. Write down the date and time it happened. Social media sites like Facebook and Twitter let you report hate speech. You can also contact organizations like the International Network Against Cyber Hate.

If you see any kind of antisemitic violence, go to a safe place and call the police.

You may feel unsafe if someone is being antisemitic towards you. Go to a safe place and talk to an adult you trust. Try to stay calm if you choose to talk to the person who is being antisemitic.

# Superheroes Against Antisemitism in the Past

**Anne Frank** was a Jewish girl who left Germany when Hitler came to power. She hid from the Nazis in Amsterdam from 1942 to 1944. She died in a concentration camp. *The Diary of Anne Frank* is the most famous book about the Holocaust.

**"In spite of everything I still believe that people are really good at heart."** –Anne Frank

**Irena Sendler** was a Polish social worker. She helped rescue over 2,000 Jewish children from the Warsaw ghetto. Even after being put in jail by the Nazis, Sendler continued her work.

**Dietrich Bonhoeffer** was a German **pastor**. Bonhoeffer spoke out against antisemitism. He worked to rescue German Jews. He died in a concentration camp in 1945.

**Pastor:** the leader of a Christian church.

"Silence in the face of evil is evil itself."
–Dietrich Bonhoeffer

23

# Superheroes Against Antisemitism Today

**Maxwell Smart** is a Holocaust survivor and author of *The Boy in the Woods*. Smart survived by hiding in the woods in the Ukraine. He and his friend Yanek saved a baby they found in the woods.

**"It will be up to you—the next generation—to pass on survivors' stories." —Maxwell Smart**

**Kathy Kacer** is a Canadian author who writes children's books about the Holocaust. Her parents were both Holocaust survivors. She was inspired by their stories.

**Lizzy Savetsky** is a New York actress and social media celebrity. In 2021, Savetsky was in Paris when a friend told her to remove her **Star of David** ring. That was when Savetsky decided to work to raise awareness about antisemitism.

KEY WORD

**Star of David:** a six-pointed star that represents Judaism.

# Ways to Support Change 1

One way to fight antisemitism is to talk openly about it. You have taken the first step towards supporting change by reading this book. Encourage your friends and family to educate themselves too.

*Hana's Suitcase* by Karen Levine is a real-life mystery about one little Jewish girl. It is a bestseller all over the world.

Try to talk to a Holocaust survivor. This will help you learn about the Holocaust and understand what survivors went through. Eliane Goldstein is a teen from Montreal. She interviews Holocaust survivors for her podcast *The Effect on Us.*

# Ways to Support Change 2

Take part in Holocaust Remembrance Day. It is called Yom Hashoah in Hebrew. In Israel, it is celebrated in the month of April. In April of 1943, the Warsaw Ghetto **Uprising** began.

KEY WORD

**Uprising:** the act of people fighting back against those in power.

About 700 young Jews took part in the Warsaw Ghetto Uprising.

Check in with your Jewish friends and family members. If they have experienced antisemitism or are hearing about it on the news, they may feel scared, angry, or confused. Ask if there is anything you can do to help them.

# Quiz

Test your knowledge of antisemitism by answering the following questions. The questions are based on what you have read in this book. The answers are listed on the bottom of the next page.

**1** What does antisemitism mean?

**2** Where were Jews forced to live during the Middle Ages?

**3** Who was the Nazi party leader who believed Jews should be killed?

**4** Which German Jewish girl wrote the most famous book about the Holocaust?

**5** Who was Dietrich Bonhoeffer?

**6** When is Holocaust Remembrance Day celebrated in Israel?

# Explore Other Level 3 Readers.

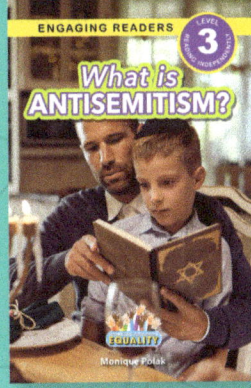

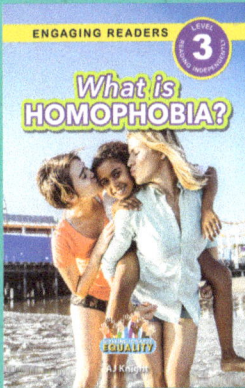

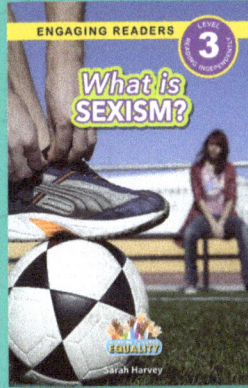

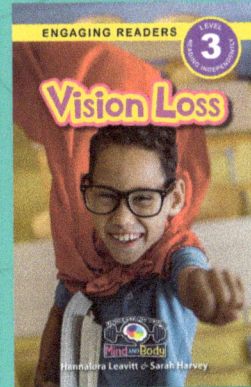

ENGAGING READERS — LEVEL 3
**What is ABLEISM?**
EQUALITY
Adelaide Wilde

ENGAGING READERS — LEVEL 3
**What is AGEISM?**
EQUALITY
Sarah Harvey

ENGAGING READERS — LEVEL 3
**What is ANTISEMITISM?**
EQUALITY
Monique Polak

ENGAGING READERS — LEVEL 3
**What is HOMOPHOBIA?**
EQUALITY
AJ Knight

ENGAGING READERS — LEVEL 3
**What is SEXISM?**
EQUALITY
Sarah Harvey

ENGAGING READERS — LEVEL 3
**Diabetes**
Mind and Body
Kit Caudron-Robinson

ENGAGING READERS — LEVEL 3
**Obesity**
Mind and Body
Kit Caudron-Robinson

ENGAGING READERS — LEVEL 3
**Autism**
Mind and Body
AJ Knight

ENGAGING READERS — LEVEL 3
**Vision Loss**
Mind and Body
Hannalora Leavitt & Sarah Harvey

Visit www.engagebooks.com/readers

**Answers:**
1. The hatred of Jews 2. In ghettos 3. Adolf Hitler
4. Anne Frank 5. A German pastor who spoke out
against antisemitism 6. In April

**31**

www.ingramcontent.com/pod-product-compliance
Lightning Source LLC
Chambersburg PA
CBHW051241020426
42331CB00016B/3477